The Gift Of Christmas
By JoAnn S. Dawson

C.S.S. Publishing Co.
Lima, Ohio

THE GIFT OF CHRISTMAS

9151 / ISBN 1-55673-352-6
PRINTED IN U.S.A.

Production Notes

Characters: Six adults, four teenagers, seven children

All of the action in the play takes place in the front of the church, with entrances made from the rear and side doors. The set is completely set up from the beginning, with lighting facilitating focus on the various scenes or vignettes. The narrator comments on the action at various times throughout.

Scriptures include: Luke 1:26-35
                          Luke 2:1-7
                          Luke 2:8-14

Hymns include: "Hark, the Herald Angels Sing"
"Silent Night"
"Joy To The World"

Performance time: 15-20 minutes

The Gift Of Christmas

Narrator: *(Enters stage right)* It is Christmas Eve, and all over town people are preparing for the Christmas Day festivities. Mothers are rushing to finish the baking, wrapping, and trimming necessary for the event, and stores are staying open for last-minute shoppers. Amid the hustle and bustle of the night, the little church in the center of town is open and prepared for any visitor who wishes to enter and find a spot of calm for a few moments at the altar. For some, on this night of activity, the scene at the altar will be a lifesaver. Watch.

7

(Mother enters from rear to stage left, with cookie tray in hand, followed by two small children and two teens, all trying to talk at once.)

First child: Can't I have one now?

Mother: No, they're too hot. I just took them out of the oven!

Second child: But that's when they taste good!

Mother: You'll have to wait until they cool down. And we have to save some for tomorrow.

Teen boy: Mom, can I have the car keys?

Teen girl: Oh, you brat! Mom, I need the car!

Mother: *(Looks at both of them)* For what?

Boy: I need to go over to Marcy's and give her her Christmas present.

Girl: You can do that tomorrow. I have to go to the mall before it closes. I forgot something!

First child: Mommy, are they cool enough yet?

Second child: Can't we just have ONE?

Mother *(to teens)***:** LOOK! Tonight we're supposed to be together — as a family. It's always been that way.

Teen boy: But, mom, we're not kids anymore.

Children: MOMMY!

(Mother looks crazed. Father enters to stage left.)

Mother *(To father)*: Can you PLEASE take over here for just an hour? I have to take a walk before I go crazy.
(To teens): You two — all right. Take the car — **together** and do what you have to do. And don't be long.

Teens: Together? But MOM!

Mother: It's together or nothing. Now go.

(Teens exit, grumbling, stage right.)

(Father exits rear, followed by kids, giving them cookies.)

(Mother exits stage left (out door).)

Narrator: And, over at the mall . . .

(Santa enters from stage right and sits, facing right, then lights switch to salesgirl entering from rear, followed by another mother and two small children. Salesgirl looks harassed, mother follows, complaining.)

Mother: But the ad said you had them!

Salesgirl: That's right, ma'am, but we ran out earlier today.

Mother: Well, whose fault is that? Don't you order adequate stock?

Salesgirl: I don't do the ordering, ma'am.

Mother *(Stage whisper)*: What am I supposed to tell these kids? I promised them!

Salesgirl *(Wearily)*: I'm sorry, ma'am.

Mother: Sorry doesn't help! Let me talk to the manager!

Salesgirl *(Getting angry)*: The manager went home. He's with his family. I'm stuck here alone. I can't help it if you leave your shopping for the last minute! I'm sorry we're out of what you want, but IT'S NOT MY FAULT! *(Looks at watch, composes herself)* It's almost closing time, ma'am.

Children: Mommy!

Mother: Okay, fine. C'mon, kids. The manager will hear from me.

(Exits stage right, past where Santa sits. Three children have entered and stand in line waiting to sit on Santa's lap. Salesgirl exits to rear, exasperated.)

(Focus on Santa: Child climbs onto his lap.)

Santa: And what would you like for Christmas?

Boy: I want a Rambo machine gun and a G.I. Joe double-bladed knife and a camouflage suit.

Santa: *(Taken aback)* Gracious, what are you going to do with all that?

Boy: I'm going to stalk the kid down the street. He's a nerd.

Santa: But wouldn't you rather try to get along with him?

Boy: Nah, he's a real spaz. His parents are poor and he probably won't even get any Christmas presents. I'm going to get everything I want, RIGHT?

Santa: *(Setting him down)* Well, we'll see.

(Boy exits rear.)

(Next child (girl) climbs on lap.)

Santa: My, what a pretty dress!

Girl: Yes, it was tailored just for me. It cost $80.

Santa: Oh, really?

Girl: Oh, yes. And the shoes were $40.

Santa: *(Hesitantly)* And, what do you want for Christmas?

Girl: Well, I just got my ears pierced. See? And I need some diamond studs. They go with everything.

Santa: I see.

Girl: And Mommy says the mini is coming back, so I'll need one of those. Designer, of course.

Santa: Mmhm. And what does Daddy say?

Girl: Oh, he doesn't live with us. He lives in Florida. I'm flying down to be with him tomorrow. Here's the address. *(Hands him a piece of paper)*

Santa: Oh, thank you.

Girl: I didn't want you to be confused over where to deliver the gifts.

(Gets down and exits rear, boy climbs up.)

Santa: And what would you . . .

Boy: My mom made me come here while she shops. I don't believe in you. I'm going to the toy department. *(Sticks out his tongue and jumps down.)*

(Santa gets up wearily and exits stage right.)

(Quiet for a moment. Lights shift to nativity scene.)

(Santa enters from stage right, drops wearily to his knees before the altar and bows his head. After a moment, he lifts his head and begins to speak to figures.)

Santa: I just don't understand it. The kids today, they're so different from when I was coming up. My family was poor. Some Christmases we couldn't afford any gifts at all. But I grew up with love. All the kids care about now is presents, presents, presents. I just don't understand it! Bows his head again.

(Salesgirl enters stage left, kneels in center of altar, bows head, and then begins to speak as Santa had.)

Salesgirl: I've got a confession to make. I'm so sorry for the way I've been acting lately, but I can't help it! Christmas just seems to be getting more hectic every year. I mean, I work so many hours and I get so tired and the people just get on my nerves so bad that I can't help being grumpy. I used to love Christmas, but now I just seem to lose my temper. I hope you can forgive me. *(Bows her head)*

(First Mother enters from rear, walks to altar and kneels to stage left. Bows her head as others had done, then speaks.)

Mother: I don't know what I'm doing here. There's still so much to do! I don't know how I got so far behind. I still haven't wrapped all the gifts, or finished baking. And we have to trim the tree later tonight. I'll end up doing most of that myself. I don't know why I do it all anyway. Nobody appreciates it. The kids are just driving me crazy this year. I'll be glad when Christmas is over. I guess I just need a break. *(Bows her head.)*

(Everything is silent for a moment, the three remain at the altar, heads bowed. Then the figure of Mary comes to life, lifting her head and looking at the woman. She speaks.)

Mary: I understand.

(The three at the altar jump in astonishment, start to get up.)

Mary: Don't be afraid. I'm here to help you.

(The three look at each other in astonishment.)

Mary: *(To woman, gently)* You, who are so troubled. Don't you see that your children are your most precious gift? Look beyond all your tasks and see your family as your joy in life. Do the gifts really need to be wrapped? Or the tree trimmed? Is the baking more important than a quiet time with your children? The gifts will be discarded, but your love will be returned a thousandfold. When I learned I was to have a child, I was frightened and confused, but I learned that this child is the greatest blessing God could have bestowed upon me. Learn to see your own children as a blessing from God.

14

Narrator: Read Luke 1:26-35

In the sixth month the angel Gabriel was sent by God to a town in Galilee called Nazareth, to a virgin engaged to a man whose name was Joseph, of the house of David. The virgin's name was Mary. And he came to her and said, "Greetings, favored one! The Lord is with you." But she was much perplexed by his words and pondered what sort of greeting this might be. The angel said to her, "Do not be afraid, Mary, for you have found favor with God. And now, you will conceive in your womb and bear a son, and you will name him Jesus. He will be great, and will be called the Son of the Most High, and the Lord God will give to him the throne of his ancestor David. He will reign over the house of Jacob forever, and of his kingdom there will be no end." Mary said to the angel. "How can this be, since I am a virgin?" The angel said to her, "The Holy Spirit will come upon you, and the power of the Most High will overshadow you; therefore the child to be born will be holy; he will be called Son of God.

Mary: *(To Santa Claus)* And you, you have such a good heart and you have been truly blessed by God in your concern and love for the children. I understand the reason for your despair, but you are the lucky one — you were raised with love, even though you had no money. Give the children time; someday they will understand. My husband and I are also poor. We have just traveled a long journey, and we had to stay the night here in the stable because there was no room in the inn. But we share the most important thing — love.

Narrator: Read Luke 2:1-7

In those days a decree went out from Emperor Augustus that all the world should be registered. This was the first registration and was taken while Quirinius was governor of Syria. All went to their own towns to be registered. Joseph also went from the town of Nazareth in Galilee to Judea, to the city of David called Bethlehem, because he was descended from the house and family of David. He went to be registered with Mary, to whom he was engaged and who was expecting a child. While they were there, the time came for her to deliver her child. And she gave birth to her firstborn son and wrapped him in bands of cloth, and laid him in a manger, because there was no place for them in the inn.

Mary: *(To the Salesgirl)* You poor child. I know what it is like to be weary and ready to give up. But be assured you are forgiven for your anger. If you will only have patience and believe, you will be forgiven all of your sins, as the Lord has promised by sending his son, your Savior. There is no longer a reason to be afraid. Be at peace.

Narrator: Reads Luke 2:8-14

In that region there were shepherds living in the fields, keeping watch over their flock by night. Then an angel of the Lord stood before them, and the glory of the Lord shone around them, and they were terrified. But the angel said to them, "Do not be afraid; for see — I am bringing you good news of great joy for all the people: to you is born this day in the city of David a Savior, who is the Messiah, the Lord. This will be a sign for you: you will find a child wrapped in bands of cloth and lying in a manger." And suddenly there was with the angel a multitude of the heavenly host, praising God and saying, "Glory to God in the highest heaven, and on earth peace among those whom he favors!"

Mary: *(To all)* Do you want to see the baby?

(She picks him up and they go up to look at him.)

(Just then, singing is heard from the rear of the church (Hark the Herald Angels Sing)*, and the rest of the characters from the play enter* (the woman's family, the three children from Santa Claus, the woman and children from the store) *singing, holding candles. All characters gather around their respective scene partners. Mary has become inanimate once more, looking down at the baby. Song ends.)*

Mother: *(To all children)* Come closer and see the baby.

(The children gather around the nativity scene, and everyone sings Silent Night, *the congregation joining in. At end of song:*

Father: *(To mother)* Feeling better?

Mother: Much better. You'd never believe what just happened. *(She looks at figure of Mary)* But I believe. Now I really believe.

(She hugs her children. Santa Claus puts his arm around the children from the store, salesgirl smiles at the second mother and children, and characters exit down center aisle, singing **Joy to the World** *with congregation.)*

The End